STORY OF
THE DINOSAURS

NAT.

Dougal Dixon

ticktock

Copyright © 2008 *ticktock* Entertainment Ltd.

First published in Great Britain by ticktock Media Ltd.,
Unit 2, Orchard Business Centre, North Farm Road, Tunbridge Wells, Kent TN2 3XF, Great Britain.

ticktock project editor: Julia Adams
ticktock project designer: Vicky Crichton

With thanks to: Jo Hanks

ISBN 978 1 84696 750 4

Printed in China

Picture credits (t=top; b=bottom; c=centre; l=left; r=right):
Main illustrations:
Lisa Anderson: 32-33.
Simon Mendez: 1, 10-11, 18-19, 22-23, 24-25, 26-27, 50-51, 54-55, 66-67 76-77, 78-79, 82-83, 86-87, 94-95, 98-99, 100-101, 102-103, 106-107.
Bob Nicholls: 44-45.
Luis Rey: 2, 6-7, 36-37, 39-39, 40-41, 42-43, 46-47, 48-49, 52-53, 56-57, 58-59, 60-61, 62-63, 64-65, 68-69, 70-71, 72-73, 74-75 84-85.
Chris Tomlin: 8-9, 12-13, 14-15, 16-17, 20-21, 28-29, 30-31, 34-35, 80-81, 88-89, 90-91, 92-93, 96-97, 104-105.

Further Images:
Hugh Lansdown/Alamy: 14. Mervyn Rees/Alamy: 19. Lisa Alderson: 5 (Mesozoic Era bottom). Amherst College Museum of Natural History: 78. Louie Psihoyos/Corbis: 53. The Field Museum: 71.
Gondwana Studios: 63. Simon Mendez: 5 (Mesozoic Era top, Palaeozoic Era top), 17. The Natural History Museum, London: 48, 81 106. Luis Rey: 5 (Mesozoic Era centre, Palaeozoic Era bottom).
Ria Novosti/Science Photo Library: 82. Tyler Olson/Shutterstock: 57. Shutterstock: 93. Chris Tomlin: 20, 31.
Ticktock Media Archive: 4TL, 4TR, 5 (Cenozoic Era), 6, 8, 11, 13, 22, 25, 27, 29, 32, 35, 37, 39, 41, 43, 45, 46, 50, 54, 59, 61, 64, 67, 68, 75, 76, 85, 86, 89, 91, 95, 98, 101, 103, 104.

CONTENTS

INTRODUCTION

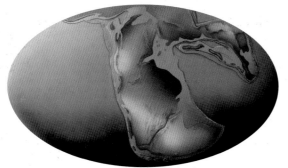

This map shows how the Earth looked at the end of the Palaeozoic Era. Most of the Earth's continents are grouped into one mass of land.

This map shows how the Earth looks today. See how different it is! The continents have split up and moved around.

This book tells the story of the evolution of animals on Earth – from the first shelled creatures to mammals. The Earth's history is divided into sections called eras, which are then divided into periods. Each period lasted for millions of years.

The chapters in this book look at the most exciting animals from each prehistoric period. The chapters are colour-coded to match the timeline on page 5.

Each animal has its own factfile, providing information on the era it lived in, its habitat, size, food, predators and amazing fossil finds.

PREHISTORIC WORLD TIMELINE

Use this timeline to trace prehistoric life. It shows how simple creatures evolved into many different kinds of animals. This took millions and millions of years. That is what MYA stands for – millions of years ago.

		PERIOD	
CENOZOIC ERA	**ICE AGE**	1.81 MYA to now QUATERNARY	This is a period of ice ages and mammals. Our direct relatives, Homo sapiens, also appear.
	ANCIENT MAMMALS	65 to 1.81 MYA TERTIARY	Giant mammals and huge hunting birds appear in this period. Our first human relatives also start to evolve.
MESOZOIC ERA	**CRETACEOUS LIFE**	145 to 65 MYA CRETACEOUS	Huge dinosaurs evolve. They have all died by the end of this period.
	JURASSIC LIFE	200 to 145 MYA JURASSIC	Large and small dinosaurs and flying creatures develop.
	TRIASSIC LIFE	250 to 200 MYA TRIASSIC	The 'Age of Dinosaurs' begins. Mammals also start to appear.
PALAEOZOIC ERA	**EARLY LIFE**	299 to 250 MYA PERMIAN	Sail-backed reptiles start to appear.
		359 to 299 MYA CARBONIFEROUS	The first reptiles appear and tropical forests develop.
		416 to 359 MYA DEVONIAN	Bony fish evolve. Trees and insects appear.
		444 to 416 MYA SILURIAN	Fish with jaws develop and land creatures appear.
		488 to 444 MYA ORDOVICIAN	Primitive fishes, trilobites, shellfish and plants evolve.
		542 to 488 MYA CAMBRIAN	First animals with skeletons appear.

PARADOXIDES

Paradoxides belonged to a group of animals called the trilobites. These were the most important sea-living animals of the Cambrian Period. There were no land-living animals at this time. Trilobites were covered in a shell made of material similar to your finger nails. They also had jointed legs. Shrimps have similar shells.

There were thousands of different kinds of trilobites. They all had a big head shield and a tail shield, and the body in between consisted of moveable segments. Some trilobites could swim, some could burrow, and others could roll up into a ball.

ANIMAL
FACTFILE

NAME: *Paradoxides* (like a puzzle)

PRONOUNCED: par-ah-dox-eye-dees

GROUP: Trilobites

WHERE IT LIVED: Canada, Europe, North Africa

WHEN IT LIVED: Early to middle Cambrian Period (542 to 513 million years ago)

LENGTH: 25 cm

SPECIAL FEATURES: Spines at the edge of each body segment

FOOD: Particles on the seabed

MAIN PREDATOR: Big arthropods

DID YOU KNOW?: *Paradoxides* was one of the first trilobites to evolve.

Paradoxides (on the right of this picture) was one of the biggest trilobites. It was hunted by even bigger animals, like the fearsome *Anomalocaris* that you see here.

7

DIPLOGRAPTUS

In the surface waters of early Palaeozoic times lived strange creatures that looked like jellyfish. These were graptolite colonies. The *Diplograptus* you see here were a type of graptolite. They had two rows of cups back to back. Each cup contained an animal. The cups were attached to a UFO-shaped unit. This is called a float. Graptolite colonies floated through the oceans anchored to their floats.

A graptolite colony looked like the blade of a saw. Each 'tooth' was a tiny cup that held an individual animal. Colonies consisted of dozens of these individuals attached together.

ANIMAL FACTFILE

NAME: *Diplograptus* (double graptolite)

PRONOUNCED: dip-low-grap-tus

GROUP: Graptolites

WHERE IT LIVED: Worldwide, in all the oceans

WHEN IT LIVED: Late Ordovician Period (461 to 444 million years ago)

LENGTH: Each string was about 10 cm

SPECIAL FEATURES: Two rows of cups back to back

FOOD: Floating organic matter

MAIN PREDATOR: None

DID YOU KNOW?: Other graptolite colonies have names based on how the cups were arranged. *Monograptus* had a single row of cups, *Tetragraptus* had four rows of cups, *Didymograptus* had two separate rows

Each tiny graptolite organism in the colony had a feathery feeding organ that trailed in the water. These gathered floating food particles.

CEPHALASPIS

Fish evolved at the beginning of the Palaeozoic Era. The first fish, like *Cephalaspis*, had no jaws, just a sucker for a mouth. *Cephalaspis* did not have much of a skeleton either – just a backbone and a skull. Its head was protected by an armoured shield, like that of a trilobite.

Cephalaspis fed from the bottom of streams and lakes. The fin on the underside of its tail kept the head downwards, and the sucker mouth could sift for food in the sand and mud.

These fossil fish were the earliest of the vertebrates – the animals with backbones.

ANIMAL FACTFILE

NAME: *Cephalaspis* (head-shield fish)

PRONOUNCED: sef-al-as-pis

GROUP: Agnathas – the jawless fish

WHERE IT LIVED: Fresh water in Northern Europe

WHEN IT LIVED: Devonian Period (416 to 359 million years ago)

LENGTH: 12 cm

SPECIAL FEATURES: *Cephalaspis* may have had electric organs on its head. They would have given an electric shock to any predator that tried to attack.

FOOD: Organic scraps on the river bed

MAIN PREDATOR: Big arthropods like giant scorpions

DID YOU KNOW?: It was from little fish like this that the whole range of modern backboned animals evolved.

11

TIKTAALIK

Among the fish of the Devonian Period, there were a few that could spend some time out of the water. These had lungs and were able to breathe air. They would not have been able to spend much time on land, but they were the first backboned animals to do so. *Tiktaalik* was one of these.

Tiktaalik was half fish, half land animal. Its fins had bones inside, like the elbow and wrist, and its head looked like a crocodile's.

ANIMAL
FACTFILE

NAME: *Tiktaalik* (big fish)

PRONOUNCED: tik-ta-lick

GROUP: Rhipidistians – with fins that could move them on land or in the water

WHERE IT LIVED: Northern Canada

WHEN IT LIVED: Late Devonian Period (375 million years ago)

LENGTH: 2.7 metres

SPECIAL FEATURES: Two pairs of fins that acted like legs, lungs that allowed it to breathe on land

FOOD: Small fish or arthropods

MAIN PREDATOR: Bigger fish

DID YOU KNOW?: There are fish today, such as the mudskipper of the tropics, that can spend time on land.

Tiktaalik lived in streams and ponds. When these dried up in hot weather, it was able to use its ability to crawl over land to find new ponds in which to live.

ICHTHYOSTEGA

Ichthyostega is the earliest amphibian that we know about. Although it had the body, legs and toes of a land-living animal, it had the head of a fish and a fishy fin on the tail. This shows that its ancestors were fish.

Ichthyostega probably had a lifestyle quite similar to the mudskipper, found in tropical regions today. Mudskippers are fish, but they have special adaptations that allow them to spend time on land.

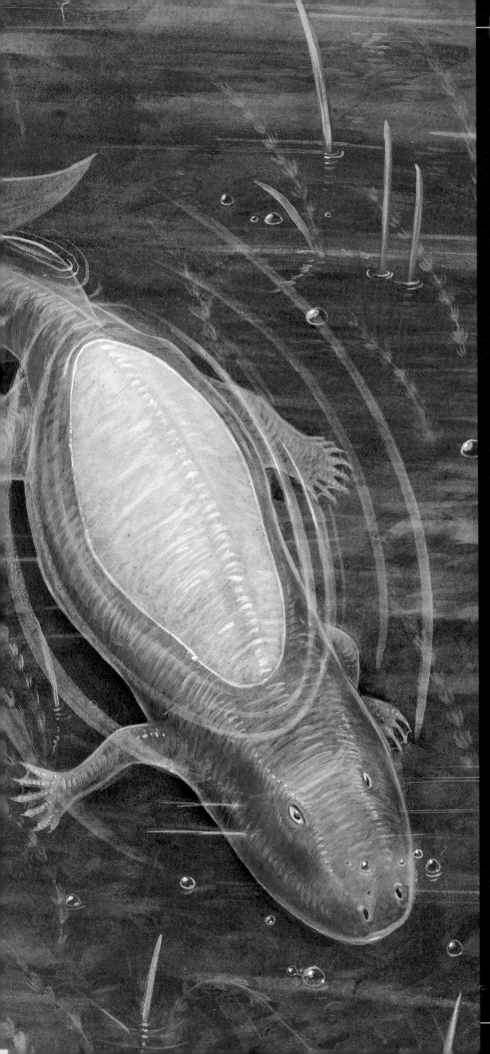

ANIMAL FACTFILE

NAME: *Ichthyostega* (fish skull)

PRONOUNCED: ick-thee-oh-stay-ga

GROUP: Labyrinthodonts – the earliest amphibians

WHERE IT LIVED: Greenland

WHEN IT LIVED: Late Devonian Period (385 – 359 million years ago)

LENGTH: 1 metre

SPECIAL FEATURES: Strong shoulders and hips, to work the legs and feet

FOOD: Insects and other small animals

MAIN PREDATOR: Big fish

DID YOU KNOW?: A strange thing about *Ichthyostega* is the number of its toes. It had eight toes on the hind foot and six on the front. Later, backboned animals would have a maximum of five toes on each foot.

Even though it was adapted to living on land, *Ichthyostega* probably spent most of its time in the water. Its feet helped it push its way through thick water weeds.

WESTLOTHIANA

The big difference between amphibians and reptiles is the fact that reptiles can lay their eggs on land. While amphibians need to lay their eggs in water, *Westlothiana* was probably able to lay its eggs on land. This would make it the first reptile.

Westlothiana looked just like a little lizard. It probably lived like one too, chasing insects through the undergrowth.

Only one fossil of *Westlothiana* has been found, and that was in a quarry, where there were also fossils of spiders, scorpions and land plants. They all lived together in swampy forests.

ANIMAL FACTFILE

NAME: *Westlothiana* (from West Lothian, the county in Scotland where it was found)

PRONOUNCED: west-low-thee-ah-na

GROUP: Possibly a very early reptile

WHERE IT LIVED: Scotland

WHEN IT LIVED: Early Carboniferous Period (338 million years ago)

LENGTH: 30 cm

SPECIAL FEATURES: Ability to lay eggs and live on land full-time

FOOD: Insects and spiders

MAIN PREDATOR: *Brontoscorpio*, a giant scorpion about 1 metre long

DID YOU KNOW?: Although we think *Westlothiana* was a reptile, its skeleton is very similar to that of an amphibian. *Westlothiana* shows how reptiles developed from amphibians.

DIMETRODON

The Permian Period was the last period of the Palaeozoic Era. When it began, deserts covered much of the Earth. *Dimetrodon* was a reptile that was well adapted to living in the hot, dry conditions.

In the cold desert mornings, *Dimetrodon* turned sideways to the Sun, and took in heat through its sail. In the heat of the day, wind passing over the sail would cool it down.

Dimetrodon had two types of teeth. This is unusual for a reptile. It had long teeth in front to cut through meat, and short ones behind to tear it into small pieces.

ANIMAL
FACTFILE

NAME: *Dimetrodon* (two kinds of teeth)

PRONOUNCED: di-met-ro-don

GROUP: Pelycosaurs

WHERE IT LIVED: Texas, USA

WHEN IT LIVED: Early Permian Period (299 to 271 million years ago)

LENGTH: 3.3 metres

SPECIAL FEATURES: Tall spines covered by skin, forming a sail on its back

FOOD: Other reptiles

MAIN PREDATOR: None

DID YOU KNOW?: Many people wrongly think that *Dimetrodon* was a dinosaur. It lived a long time before the dinosaurs and was not related at all.

LYCAENOPS

Lycaenops had a long skull with sharp teeth and long legs for running fast. It may have lived in packs. Many scientists think it looked and behaved rather like a wolf. Permian reptiles like *Lycaenops* were the distant ancestors of the mammals.

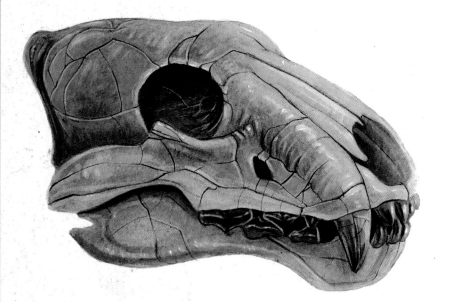

Lycaenops had killing teeth at the front of its mouth, and meat-shredding teeth at the back. Modern wolves use their teeth in the same way.

ANIMAL
FACTFILE

NAME: *Lycaenops* (looking like a wolf)

PRONOUNCED: lie-kee-nops

GROUP: Gorgonopsians – one of the groups of mammal-like reptiles

WHERE IT LIVED: South Africa

WHEN IT LIVED: Late Permian Period (260 to 250 million years ago)

LENGTH: 1 metre

SPECIAL FEATURES: Dog-like or wolf-like teeth

FOOD: Other reptiles

MAIN PREDATOR: Bigger meat-eating reptiles

DID YOU KNOW?: *Lycaenops* had legs close to its body (like mammals today) not out to the side (like a crocodile's legs). This helped it to run faster than the other animals of the time.

There were bigger hunting reptiles around at the time, but *Lycaenops* would have been a fierce predator of smaller reptiles.

PSEPHODERMA

By the time of the Triassic Period, there were all kinds of animals living on land. There were also many that returned to the sea and found it easier to live there. The placodonts were a group of reptiles that lived in the sea and ate shellfish. *Psephoderma* had a long, pointed snout and strong jaws. It was ideally adapted for picking shellfish off reefs and crushing them with its broad teeth.

Psephoderma

Placochelys

Psephoderma had a shell on its back and looked rather like a turtle. You can see the shell in this fossil. However, *Psephoderma* was not closely related to the turtles. It evolved a similar shape and shell because it had a similar lifestyle.

Henodus

ANIMAL FACTFILE

NAME: *Psephoderma* (rough skin)

PRONOUNCED: sef-oh-der-ma

GROUP: Placodonts – a group of swimming shellfish-eaters

WHERE IT LIVED: The seas around Southern Europe

WHEN IT LIVED: Late Triassic Period (228 to 200 million years ago)

LENGTH: 1.5 metres

SPECIAL FEATURES: Turtle-like shell on the back, and another over the hips

FOOD: Shellfish

MAIN PREDATOR: Other big swimming reptiles and shark-like fish

DID YOU KNOW?: Not all placodonts had shells. Some looked like giant newts. One relative, *Placodus*, was 2 metres long.

The placodonts in this picture all had armoured backs. Their shells would have protected them from the other sea-living reptiles of the time, some of which were much bigger and fiercer.

23

NOTHOSAURUS

Nothosaurus was one of the earliest sea-living reptilian hunters. Its feet were webbed, like those of a seal, and it had quite a long neck and long toothy jaws – just right for snatching at fish. It had a long tail to help it to swim. Even though *Nothosaurus* spent most of its time in the water, it had to come to the surface to breathe.

Ceresiosaurus

There were several types of nothosaur. *Lariosaurus* was one of the smallest, about 60 cm long. *Ceresiosaurus* and *Nothosaurus* were bigger, and better adapted to life in the sea. They had long necks that made it easier to catch fish, and feet that were used like paddles.

Lariosaurus

Nothosaurus

ANIMAL
FACTFILE

NAME: *Nothosaurus* (false lizard)

PRONOUNCED: noth-oh-sawr-us

GROUP: Nothosaurs

WHERE IT LIVED: From Europe and north Africa to China

WHEN IT LIVED: The whole of the Triassic Period (250 to 200 million years ago)

LENGTH: 3 metres

SPECIAL FEATURES: Webbed feet and long sharp teeth

FOOD: Fish and smaller swimming reptiles

MAIN PREDATOR: Sharks

DID YOU KNOW?: *Nothosaurus* did not spend all of its time at sea. The bones of its legs show that it was capable of clambering about on land. It would have needed to come ashore in order to lay eggs.

Fossils of nothosaurs – the group to which *Nothosaurus* belonged – have been found all over the world. *Nothosaurus* was the most common and widespread of them.

SHONISAURUS

Among the reptiles that returned to the sea, probably the most famous are the ichthyosaurs – the 'fish-lizards'. These were so well adapted to living in the sea that they could not have spent any time on land. Some of the earliest forms, like *Shonisaurus* were enormous – truly whale-sized.

Shonisaurus was the biggest sea animal of the Triassic Period. One species, *Shonisaurus sikanniensis*, was 21 metres long. Its fossil was found in a remote river bank in Canada.

ANIMAL
FACTFILE

NAME: *Shonisaurus* (lizard from the Shoshone Mountains, Nevada, USA)

PRONOUNCED: shon-ee-sawr-us

GROUP: Ichthyosaurs — the fish-lizards

WHERE IT LIVED: The sea which covered parts of the USA and Canada in Triassic times

WHEN IT LIVED: Late Triassic Period (228 to 200 million years ago)

LENGTH: 15 metres

SPECIAL FEATURES: Its size! It was the biggest ichthyosaur known

FOOD: Fish and sea-going invertebrates, like ammonites

MAIN PREDATOR: None

DID YOU KNOW?: Scientists think that *Shonisaurus* only had teeth when it was young. Adults were toothless.

This fossil shows a typical ichthyosaur. These reptiles were strong swimmers with streamlined bodies that enabled them to slide effortlessly through the water. The large paddles were actually fingers that had become joined together.

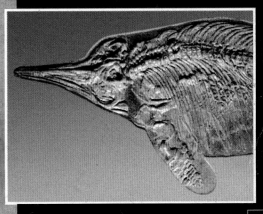

EUDIMORPHODON

Towards the end of the Triassic Period
some reptiles mastered the skill of
flying. Until then there had
been a few lizard-like reptiles
that were able to glide for
long distances. But now the
pterosaurs appeared – reptiles that
could fly by flapping their wings
like birds. *Eudimorphodon* was
one of the first of the pterosaurs.

The pointed front teeth of *Eudimorphodon* were ideal
for catching fish as it flew low over the
surface of quiet lagoons. The smaller
teeth at the back of the mouth
would have gripped the slippery prey firmly
while it was taken back to land to be eaten.

Like other pterosaurs, *Eudimorphodon* had wings that were supported by a single, long fourth finger. It also had a long stiff tail that it used for steering.

ANIMAL
FACTFILE

NAME: *Eudimorphodon* (with two very differently shaped teeth)

PRONOUNCED: you-dee-morf-oh-don

GROUP: Pterosaurs — the flying reptiles

WHERE IT LIVED: Italy

WHEN IT LIVED: Late Triassic Period (228 to 200 million years ago)

BODY LENGTH: 0.6 metres

WINGSPAN: 1 metre

SPECIAL FEATURES: Two different types of teeth

FOOD: Fish

MAIN PREDATOR: Big fish and big reptiles

DID YOU KNOW?: One fossil of a close relative, *Preondactylus*, was found as a bundle of bones, coughed up by a fish that had eaten it over 200 million years ago.

ARIZONASAURUS

The fiercest meat-eaters in Triassic
times were big land-living rauisuchians
like *Arizonasaurus*, distant relatives
of crocodiles. They did not
crawl, like modern crocodiles,
but walked on straight legs,
like dogs. They prowled
around the desert
landscapes hunting,
the big plant-eating
reptiles that lived
in the oases
of the time.

The sail may have kept
Arizonasaurus warm
by taking in heat from the
Sun in the chilly mornings.
This would have made it
more active than its slow-
moving prey, and would
have helped it to hunt.

The first fossils of *Arizonasaurus* were found in 1947, but the scientists of the time thought they were just dinosaur bones. It was not until 2000 that it was realised the fossils came from a type of rauisuchian, not a dinosaur. The new animal was named *Arizonasaurus*.

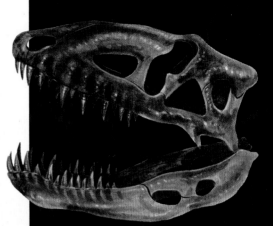

ANIMAL
FACTFILE

NAME: *Arizonasaurus* (lizard from Arizona)

PRONOUNCED: a-riz-oh-na-sawr-us

GROUP: Rauisuchians — a group of land-living crocodiles

WHERE IT LIVED: Arizona, USA

WHEN IT LIVED: Middle Triassic Period (245 to 228 million years ago)

LENGTH: 3 metres

SPECIAL FEATURES: Tall sail on its back

FOOD: Plant-eating reptiles

MAIN PREDATOR: None

DID YOU KNOW?: *Arizonasaurus* looked rather like *Dimetrodon*, an earlier reptile with a sail on its back. In fact, these two reptiles are not closely related. They look the same because their lifestyles were similar.

EORAPTOR

In Late Triassic times, many of the big land animals were relatives of crocodiles and other reptiles. The first dinosaurs were really quite small. *Eoraptor* was only the size of a large turkey, but it was an ancestor of the huge and magnificent dinosaurs to come.

This copy of an *Eoraptor* skull shows its long jaws and sharp teeth, just like those of later meat-eating dinosaurs. *Eoraptor* was also the same general shape as later predators. Its small body was carried on two strong hind legs. The arms were smaller, with grasping fingers, and its neck was long and flexible. A long heavy tail helped the dinosaur to balance.

ANIMAL FACTFILE

NAME: *Eoraptor* (early hunter)

PRONOUNCED: ee-oh-rap-tor

GROUP: Theropod dinosaurs

WHERE IT LIVED: Patagonia in South America

WHEN IT LIVED: Late Triassic Period (228 million years ago)

LENGTH: 1 metre

SPECIAL FEATURES: The earliest dinosaur known

FOOD: Small animals and insects

MAIN PREDATOR: Big land-living rauisuchians

DID YOU KNOW?: Later meat-eating dinosaurs had three, or even two, fingers on the hand. Like its ancestors, *Eoraptor* still had five, although two of them were tiny. Changes like this help scientists to trace the evolution of dinosaurs.

Although *Eoraptor* was not very big, it was very active and fierce. It hunted small creatures of the time, such as reptiles and insects.

UNAYSAURUS

Dinosaurs quickly evolved into two groups: the meat-eaters and the plant-eaters. *Unaysaurus* was one of the earliest of the plant-eating groups. Like other dinosaurs of the time, *Unaysaurus* was smaller than many other animals around. Its later descendants were very much bigger – they were the massive long-necked sauropods such as *Brachiosaurus*.

Unaysaurus had teeth that were roughly serrated, like vegetable graters. It ate plants that grew on the ground, and probably also stood on its hind legs to reach leaves high up in trees.

Part of the *Unaysaurus* skeleton found in Brazil in 2004. From this, scientists can see that the hind legs of *Unaysaurus* were much longer and heavier than its front legs. This suggests that it was able to spend a lot of time on its hind legs.

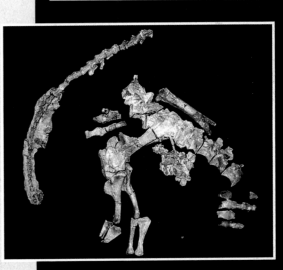

ANIMAL
FACTFILE

NAME: *Unaysaurus* (Black Water lizard, named after the area where it was found)

PRONOUNCED: you-na-sawr-us

GROUP: Prosauropod dinosaurs

WHERE IT LIVED: Brazil

WHEN IT LIVED: Late Triassic Period (228 to 200 million years ago)

LENGTH: 2.4 metres

SPECIAL FEATURES: The earliest known of the long-necked plant-eaters

FOOD: Leaves and ferns

MAIN PREDATOR: Big land-living crocodiles and early dinosaurs

DID YOU KNOW?: *Unaysaurus* was closely related to other dinosaurs found in North America, Germany and China. This shows the same kinds of animals lived all over the world at that time.

COELOPHYSIS

The early meat-eating dinosaurs may have been small, but some of them made up for this in cunning. *Coelophysis* was one of the earliest of the meat-eaters. There is evidence that it hunted in packs. Pack-hunting animals can successfully hunt beasts much larger than themselves.

Coelophysis was probably a scavenger, as well as a hunter, and ate almost anything it could find. Many types of fish and reptiles have been found in its stomach.

Two forms of *Coelophysis* fossil have been found. One form is thinner and more delicate than the other. It is thought they are male and female dinosaurs.

ANIMAL FACTFILE

NAME: *Coelophysis* (hollow form)

PRONOUNCED: see-low-fye-sis

GROUP: Theropod dinosaurs

WHERE IT LIVED: Arizona and New Mexico

WHEN IT LIVED: Late Triassic Period (228 to 216 million years ago)

LENGTH: 3 metres — but most was neck and tail, and its body was about the same size as a fox

SPECIAL FEATURES: Lived and hunted in packs

FOOD: Other reptiles

MAIN PREDATOR: Big land-living rauisuchians

DID YOU KNOW?: A fossil skull of *Coelophysis* was taken on the space shuttle *Endeavor* in 1998. It was the first dinosaur in space!

CYNOGNATHUS

One group of reptiles became very similar to mammals in Triassic times. They were probably warm-blooded, like mammals, and had a similar body shape. They might have even had fur. Eventually, this group evolved into the mammals themselves, in the late Triassic. *Cynognathus* was one of the most mammal-like of these reptiles.

Scientists think *Cynognathus* was covered in fur, because the bones of its snout show tiny pits where whiskers would have been. Only furry animals have whiskers.

The skull of the *Cynognathus* is very similar to the skull of a mammal. Only the shape of the jaw shows that it was actually a reptile.

ANIMAL FACTFILE

NAME: *Cynognathus* (dog jaw)

PRONOUNCED: sy-nog-nay-thus

GROUP: Therapsids — a group of mammal-like reptiles

WHERE IT LIVED: South Africa

WHEN IT LIVED: Middle Triassic Period (245 to 228 million years ago)

LENGTH: 1.5 metres

SPECIAL FEATURES: Teeth like a dog, with nipping incisors at the front, stabbing canines at the side, and meat-shearing molars at the back

FOOD: Other animals

MAIN PREDATOR: The big land-living rauisuchians

DID YOU KNOW?: The jawbone of *Cynognathus*, or something closely related, has been found in Antarctica. This shows that Africa and Antarctica were joined together in Triassic times.

39

ICHTHYOSAURUS

In the Mesozoic Era, the seas were full of swimming reptiles. One of the most common were the ichthyosaurs, or 'fish-lizards'. When they first evolved, ichthyosaurs were big whale-like animals.

By the time of the Jurassic Period, the ichthyosaurs, including *Ichthyosaurus* itself, were smaller and more dolphin-like.

Ichthyosaurs gave birth to live young. They did not need to come ashore to lay eggs. We know this because there are fossils of baby ichthyosaurs preserved while being born.

Ichthyosaurus and the other ichthyosaurs were the fastest hunters in the Jurassic seas. Like modern dolphins, they could chase and catch the fastest of the fish and squid-like animals that lived at the time.

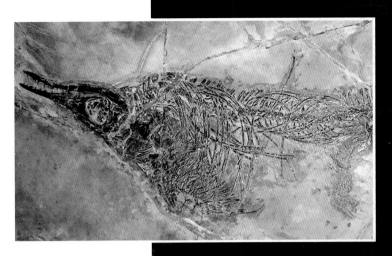

ANIMAL
FACTFILE

NAME: *Ichthyosaurus* (fish lizard)

PRONOUNCED: ik-thee-oh-sawr-us

GROUP: Ichthyosaurs

WHERE IT LIVED: Worldwide

WHEN IT LIVED: Early Jurassic Period (200 to 176 million years ago)

LENGTH: 2.1 metres

SPECIAL FEATURES: Most streamlined and fish-like of the reptiles

FOOD: Fish and cephalopods

MAIN PREDATOR: Pliosaurs

DID YOU KNOW?: Usually we do not know what the soft, fleshy parts of a fossil animal look like, but some fossils of *Ichthyosaurus* still have their fins preserved.

CRYPTOCLIDUS

The plesiosaurs were some of the most
important swimming reptiles of Jurassic times.
There were two types – those with long necks
and those with short necks. *Cryptoclidus* was
a long-necked plesiosaur.

"Like a snake
threaded through
a turtle" was the
description of a long-
necked plesiosaur given
by one early palaeontologist.
The long neck, broad body and
paddles give this impression.

Cryptoclidus flew through the water. Its front paddles worked like wings, and the hind paddles as stabilisers. It could reach around for food with its long neck.

ANIMAL FACTFILE

NAME: *Cryptoclidus* (hidden collar bone)

PRONOUNCED: crip-tow-cly-dus

GROUP: Long-necked plesiosaurs

WHERE IT LIVED: Europe

WHEN IT LIVED: Late Jurassic Period (161 to 145 million years ago)

LENGTH: 8 metres

SPECIAL FEATURES: Long pointed teeth, ideal for catching slippery prey

FOOD: Fish and squid

MAIN PREDATOR: Short-necked plesiosaurs, such as *Liopleurodon*

DID YOU KNOW?: Fossils form more easily in the sea than on land. So fossils from swimming reptiles are more common than fossils from some land animals. Scientists were studying plesiosaur fossils long before they discovered dinosaur fossils.

LIOPLEURODON

The biggest reptiles of the Jurassic seas, and probably the biggest meat-eating animals of all time, were the short-necked plesiosaurs. They had very long jaws, like a crocodile. The biggest of them was the huge *Liopleurodon*.

Liopleurodon might have been able to sink in the water by swallowing stones, and float by spitting them out. Its streamlined body meant that, despite its size, it could swim as fast as any other sea reptile of the time. Its head was big enough to swallow you whole, had you been around.

ANIMAL FACTFILE

NAME: *Liopleurodon* (smooth-sided tooth)

PRONOUNCED: lie-oh-ploor-oh-don

GROUP: Short-necked plesiosaurs

WHERE IT LIVED: Northern Europe

WHEN IT LIVED: Late Jurassic Period (161 to 145 million years ago)

LENGTH: 15 metres

SPECIAL FEATURES: The biggest sea reptile of the time

FOOD: Other sea reptiles

MAIN PREDATOR: None

DID YOU KNOW?: Short-necked plesiosaurs ranged in size from penguin-sized to the size of a sperm whale. *Liopleurodon* was one of the biggest.

This is the tooth of a *Liopleurodon*. It is about 20 cm long. Bite marks from *Liopleurodon* have been found on the bones of ichthyosaurs and other plesiosaurs, showing that *Liopleurodon* was a fierce predator.

45

PTERODACTYLUS

The skies were full of flying animals in late Jurassic times, including insects and the first birds. However, the most important flying animals were actually reptiles, the pterosaurs. There were two groups, the long-tailed pterosaurs and the short-tailed pterosaurs. *Pterodactylus* was a short-tailed pterosaur.

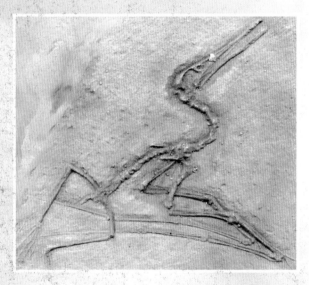

Many well-preserved pterosaur fossils have been found. Here you can clearly see the bones of the spine and neck. In some fossils, it is even possible to see the wing membrane.

ANIMAL FACTFILE

NAME: *Pterodactylus* (wing finger)

PRONOUNCED: ter-oh-dak-til-us

GROUP: Pterodactyloids — the short-tailed pterosaurs

WHERE IT LIVED: Northern Europe and Africa

WHEN IT LIVED: Late Jurassic Period (161 to 145 million years ago)

WINGSPAN: 1 metre

SPECIAL FEATURES: Broad wings, a short tail and a long neck

FOOD: Fish and small reptiles

MAIN PREDATOR: Larger pterosaurs

DID YOU KNOW?: The first pterosaurs found were thought to have been swimming animals — scientists thought that the wings were fins.

There were many different species of *Pterodactylus*. Each one was adapted to eat a particular food. Smaller ones were probably insect-eaters, bigger ones (like this one here) probably ate fish or small lizards.

HETERODONTOSAURUS

Heterodontosaurus looks like a fierce meat-eater. But this was just an aggressive pose. It was, in fact, a plant-eating dinosaur that probably scared away its predators by pretending to be fearsome. If that did not work, it was small and light enough to run away quickly.

Look closely at this skull fossil, and you can see a long side tusk (at the right). It is possible that only the male *Heterodontosaurus* had these. Maybe they were used during the mating season, to scare away rivals. Like other ornithopods, *Heterodontosaurus* had a bird-like beak at the front of its mouth.

ANIMAL
FACTFILE

NAME: *Heterodontosaurus* (lizard with differently shaped teeth)

PRONOUNCED: het-er-oh-don-toh-sawr-us

GROUP: Ornithopod dinosaurs

WHERE IT LIVED: South Africa

WHEN IT LIVED: Early Jurassic Period (200 to 190 million years ago)

LENGTH: 1.2 metres

SPECIAL FEATURES: Three kinds of teeth — nipping teeth inside the beak at the front, tusks at the side, and grinding teeth at the back

FOOD: Plants

MAIN PREDATOR: Meat-eating dinosaurs and crocodiles

DID YOU KNOW?: *Heterodontosaurus* had five-fingered hands, but two of the fingers were tiny.

Heterodontosaurus has one of the best-preserved dinosaur skeletons known. The fossils were found in South Africa in 1966. The skeleton shows that it had long hind legs used for running, and short arms with little hands for grasping.

STEGOSAURUS

One of the most recognisable of the armoured dinosaurs was *Stegosaurus*. It had a double row of plates down the back. These were either covered in horn and used for defence, or covered in skin and used to keep the dinosaur warm – we are not yet sure which.

Stegosaurus may have used its plates to keep warm. When it was cold, it would have stood sideways to the Sun, so sunlight could warm its plates. When *Stegosaurus* was hot, it could have cooled off by holding the plates into the wind.

ANIMAL
FACTFILE

NAME: *Stegosaurus* (roofed lizard)

PRONOUNCED: steg-oh-sawr-us

GROUP: Thyreophoran dinosaurs

WHERE IT LIVED: Mid-west of the United States

WHEN IT LIVED: Late Jurassic Period (156 to 145 million years ago)

LENGTH: 9 metres

SPECIAL FEATURES: Two pairs of spikes on tail for defence

FOOD: Plants

MAIN PREDATOR: Big meat-eating dinosaurs like *Allosaurus*

DID YOU KNOW?: The brain of *Stegosaurus* is so small that people used to think it must have had a second brain in its hips to control the legs and tail.

Stegosaurus probably spent most of its time on four legs. However, its hips and hind legs were very strong, showing that it could rear up on its hind legs, to eat from the low branches of trees.

BRACHIOSAURUS

One of the biggest dinosaurs was *Brachiosaurus*.
It was one of the long-necked plant-eating sauropods.
There were many types of big sauropods in the Late
Jurassic. Some were adapted for grazing the plants
that grew close to the ground. Others, like
Brachiosaurus, were tall, so they could
eat the leaves and needles
from high trees.

Brachiosaurus
is one of the
biggest land-
living animals known. However, the bones of
Brachiosaurus weren't as heavy as you might think.
The bones were hollow, which meant they could
be long and lightweight at the same time.

ANIMAL
FACTFILE

NAME: *Brachiosaurus* (arm lizard)

PRONOUNCED: brack-ee-oh-sawr-us

GROUP: Sauropod dinosaurs

WHERE IT LIVED: East Africa and the mid-west of the United States

WHEN IT LIVED: Mid to Late Jurassic Period (156 to 145 million years ago)

LENGTH: 24 metres

SPECIAL FEATURES: Long neck, small head. The tail was 7.5 metres long – relatively short for a sauropod.

FOOD: Leaves from trees

MAIN PREDATOR: Big meat-eating dinosaurs like *Allosaurus*

DID YOU KNOW?: *Brachiosaurus* fossils have been found in both Africa and North America, showing that the two continents were close together in Late Jurassic times.

Can you picture how big *Brachiosaurus* was? This photo might help. *Brachiosaurus* was over 12 metres tall, about the height of a 4-storey building.

ALLOSAURUS

The biggest and fiercest of the meat-eating dinosaurs in the Late Jurassic Period was *Allosaurus*. It was big enough to hunt the largest of the plant-eating sauropods, although, like lions and tigers today, it probably concentrated on the young, the old and the injured.

Over 40 skeletons of *Allosaurus* have been found in a single quarry in Utah, USA. Most of the *Allosaurus* skeletons that we see in museums today have come from this site.

With the big claws on its three-fingered hands, *Allosaurus* could seize its prey easily. It would have killed the animal with its steak-knife teeth. After it had finished eating, there would have been plenty left over for smaller scavenging dinosaurs and pterosaurs.

ANIMAL FACTFILE

NAME: *Allosaurus* (different lizard)

PRONOUNCED: al-oh-sawr-us

GROUP: Theropod dinosaurs

WHERE IT LIVED: Western parts of the United States

WHEN IT LIVED: Late Jurassic Period (156 to 145 million years ago)

LENGTH: 11.5 metres

SPECIAL FEATURES: The biggest land-living meat-eater of the time

FOOD: Big plant-eating dinosaurs, like *Stegosaurus* or *Brachiosaurus*

MAIN PREDATOR: None

DID YOU KNOW?: *Allosaurus* weighed around 5 tonnes – about the weight of an elephant. There were several smaller species, some weighing as little as 1 tonne – which is still heavy.

GUANLONG

The most famous meat-eating dinosaur of all time must be *Tyrannosaurus*. *Guanlong* was one of its earliest relatives. This dinosaur was quite small in comparison to its famous relatives. But it was just as fierce a hunter, although it preyed on smaller animals.

Most active animals, such as mammals and birds, are warm-blooded. Hair or feathers help them to control their body temperature. Scientists think that the small, meat-eating dinosaurs were active enough to have been warm-blooded, and so probably had a feathery covering.

ANIMAL FACTFILE

NAME: *Guanlong* (crowned dragon)

PRONOUNCED: gwan-long

GROUP: Theropod dinosaurs

WHERE IT LIVED: China

WHEN IT LIVED: Late Jurassic Period (160 million years ago)

LENGTH: 3 metres

SPECIAL FEATURES: The earliest tyrannosaur known

FOOD: Other dinosaurs

MAIN PREDATOR: Bigger meat-eating dinosaurs

DID YOU KNOW?: Until *Guanlong* was discovered, scientists thought that tyrannosaurs only lived in Cretaceous times.

Guanlong had a crest on its head. It would have been used for signalling to other dinosaurs. Otherwise it was very similar in shape to the *Tyrannosaurus* skull you see here.

QUETZALCOATLUS

Towards the end of the Cretaceous Period, the flying reptiles – the pterosaurs – became truly enormous. *Quetzalcoatlus* was amongst the biggest, and was almost the size of a small aeroplane. Despite its huge wingspan, it would not have weighed much more than an adult human.

Most pterosaurs lived near the sea, where they hunted for fish. *Quetzalcoatlus* was different, it lived far inland. It may have been a scavenger, feeding on the bodies of dinosaurs that had died on the open plains. It would have soared like a vulture and spotted dead animals from far away.

ANIMAL
FACTFILE

NAME: *Quetzalcoatlus* (after the ancient Mexican god, Quetzalcoatl, that took the form of a flying serpent)

PRONOUNCED: ket-sal-koh-aht-lus

GROUP: Pterosaurs

WHERE IT LIVED: Texas, USA

WHEN IT LIVED: Late Cretaceous Period (84 to 65 million years ago)

WINGSPAN: 10.6 metres

SPECIAL FEATURES: Broad wings, long neck, very long jaws

FOOD: Possibly carrion

MAIN PREDATOR: None

DID YOU KNOW?: *Quetzalcoatlus* is one of the biggest ever flying animals. Today, the bird with the largest wingspan is the albatross, which has a wingspan of 3.3 metres.

A complete skeleton of *Quetzalcoatlus* has never been found. We have a good idea of what it looked like from the few fossils that have been found and put together, like this one.

ELASMOSAURUS

The plesiosaurs were swimming reptiles, and most had very long necks. *Elasmosaurus* had a neck that was 7.5 metres long – more than half of its total length. It cruised the warm waters of the shallow sea that stretched across North America at the end of the Cretaceous Period, hunting fish that were in great supply there.

The way the vertebrae of the neck are joined together suggests that *Elasmosaurus* swam near the surface of the water and reached down to catch its prey. The long neck probably also allowed it to reach out and snatch fish, without moving its body too far or too quickly.

Elasmosaurus had tiny nostrils which were not used for breathing, but to sense prey moving in the water. To breathe, *Elasmosaurus* would have swum to the surface of the sea to take in air through its mouth.

ANIMAL
FACTFILE

NAME: *Elasmosaurus* (thin plate lizard)

PRONOUNCED: eh-laz-mo-sawr-us

GROUP: Plesiosaurs

WHERE IT LIVED: Kansas, USA

WHEN IT LIVED: Late Cretaceous Period (84 to 65 million years ago)

LENGTH: 13 metres

SPECIAL FEATURES: Long neck with 71 vertebrae (we humans have only 7)

FOOD: Fish

MAIN PREDATOR: Big swimming reptiles like *Tylosaurus*

DID YOU KNOW?: The first scientist to study *Elasmosaurus* built the skeleton wrongly. He put the head on the tail end, thinking the short tail was the neck and the long neck was the tail.

IGUANODON

Iguanodon was one of the first dinosaurs to be discovered. Scientists studying its fossil thought that it looked like a big reptile. Most big reptiles are meat-eaters, but the teeth of this fossil showed it ate plants. The iguana, a plant-eating lizard, has teeth similar to *Iguanodon*. So the plant-eating dinosaur was named *Iguanodon* – 'iguana tooth'.

Scientists used to think that *Iguanodon* stood upright, resting on its tail like a kangaroo. Now they think that it usually walked on all fours, and only reached up to feed.

Iguanodon was common in northern Europe, but it had close relatives all over the world. *Muttaburrasaurus* lived in Australia, while big-nosed *Altirhinus* (right) lived in Mongolia.

ANIMAL
FACTFILE

NAME: *Iguanodon* (iguana tooth)

PRONOUNCED: ig-wan-oh-don

GROUP: Ornithopod dinosaurs

WHERE IT LIVED: Northern Europe

WHEN IT LIVED: Early Cretaceous Period (135 to 125 million years ago)

LENGTH: 9 metres

SPECIAL FEATURES: First finger had a big horny spike for defence, and for ripping trees

FOOD: Plants

MAIN PREDATOR: Big meat-eating dinosaurs, like *Neovenator*

DID YOU KNOW?: *Iguanodon's* fifth finger was small and flexible, and used like a thumb.

STYGIMOLOCH

At the end of the Cretaceous Period, a group of dinosaurs called the marginocephalians evolved. One group of marginocephalians was the boneheads. These goat-sized animals had a massive lump of bone on their head that they used as a battering ram. One of the strangest-looking boneheads was *Stygimoloch*.

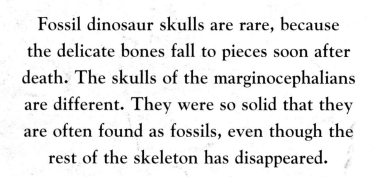

Fossil dinosaur skulls are rare, because the delicate bones fall to pieces soon after death. The skulls of the marginocephalians are different. They were so solid that they are often found as fossils, even though the rest of the skeleton has disappeared.

ANIMAL FACTFILE

NAME: *Stygimoloch* (horned devil from the river of death)

PRONOUNCED: stig-ih-moe-lock

GROUP: Marginocephalians

WHERE IT LIVED: Canada and the mid-west of the United States

WHEN IT LIVED: Late Cretaceous Period (71 to 65 million years ago)

LENGTH: 2.7 metres

SPECIAL FEATURES: The stiff, straight tail was used for balance

FOOD: Plants

MAIN PREDATOR: Big meat-eating dinosaurs like *Tyrannosaurus*

DID YOU KNOW?: All boneheads used their heavy heads as weapons to head-butt their rivals.

Stygimoloch had a spectacular number of horns around its skull. These would have been used to make it look bigger and fiercer than it actually was, to scare away predators.

TRICERATOPS

Triceratops is one of the most recognisable of the dinosaurs. It had a huge rhinoceros-like body and a massive bony head with three horns pointing forward. It roamed the plains of North America in herds at the very end of the 'Age of Dinosaurs'.

Triceratops had a big beak at the front of its mouth. It used this to snip off shoots and twigs from bushes and trees. It had chopping teeth at the back of its mouth, and cheek pouches to hold its food while chewing it.

Triceratops was a ceratopsian dinosaur. There were many types of ceratopsian dinosaurs. They all looked very similar to one another, except for the number and arrangement of horns on the head. Some had a single horn on the nose, some had a pair of horns over the eyes, and some only had horns on the armoured shield around the neck.

ANIMAL
FACTFILE

NAME: *Triceratops* (three-horned face)

PRONOUNCED: try-sair-oh-tops

GROUP: Marginocephalians (ceratopsian group)

WHERE IT LIVED: North America

WHEN IT LIVED: Late Cretaceous Period (72 to 65 million years ago)

LENGTH: 7.5 metres

SPECIAL FEATURES: A solid armoured shield around the neck

FOOD: Tough plants

MAIN PREDATOR: Big meat-eating dinosaurs like *Tyrannosaurus*

DID YOU KNOW?: *Triceratops* was one of the last dinosaurs to evolve before all dinosaurs became extinct 65 million years ago.

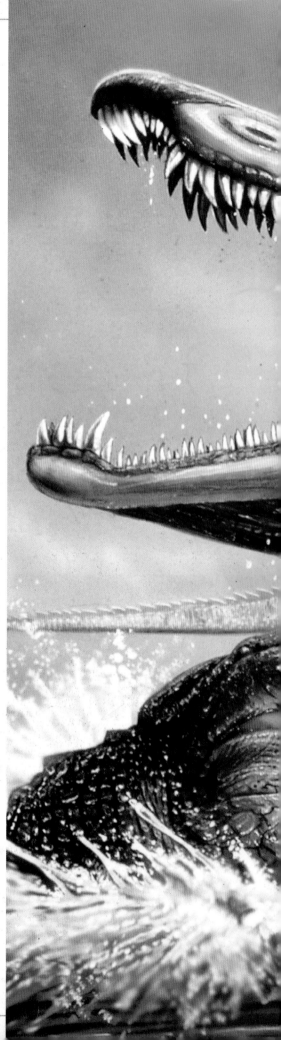

SUCHOMIMUS

This frightening creature belongs to a group of dinosaurs called the spinosaurids. These fish-eating creatures lived in the Early Cretaceous period. *Suchomimus* would have used its claws to hook the fish out of water, throw them onto the land, and snap them up in its long jaws.

Suchomimus was a very powerful dinosaur. Its skull was crocodile-like, with a long snout and a large number of sharp teeth. These would have allowed it to grasp the slippery surface of a fish's scaly skin.

Suchomimus was a fierce predator, but even it was hunted by bigger creatures. In this picture, a gigantic crocodile lunges out of the water to attack *Suchomimus*.

ANIMAL FACTFILE

NAME: *Suchomimus* (crocodile mimic)

PRONOUNCED: soo-cho-my-mas

GROUP: Theropods

WHERE IT LIVED: North Africa

WHEN IT LIVED: Early Cretaceous Period (110 to 100 million years ago)

LENGTH: 11 metres

SPECIAL FEATURES: Long narrow crocodile-like jaws

FOOD: Fish

MAIN PREDATOR: A gigantic crocodile called *Sarcosuchus*

DID YOU KNOW?: The spinosaurids were a widespread group. Closely related dinosaurs have been found in England, Thailand and Brazil.

BUITRERAPTOR

Scientists used to think that the small, fast, meat-eating dinosaurs that looked like birds only lived in Europe, Africa and North America. Then, in 2005, scientists found the remains of *Buitreraptor* in South America. In the Cretaceous Period, South America was an island, like Australia today. This means that the ancestors of *Buitreraptor* and the rest of the bird-like dinosaurs must have existed before the continents broke up, maybe 200 million years ago.

Scientists have not found fossilised feathers with *Buitreraptor*. They think it had feathers because its long legs and light build show that it was very active, and so probably warm-blooded. Most warm-blooded animals have fur or feathers to keep themselves warm. Relatives of *Buitreraptor* had feathers, so it is likely that *Buitreraptor* did, too.

Several skeletons of *Buitreraptor* were found in the same general area, in South America. It looks as though it was quite a common animal at that time. From the many remains, scientists have been able to build up a complete skeleton.

ANIMAL FACTFILE

NAME: *Buitreraptor* (vulture hunter)

PRONOUNCED: bewt-re-rap-tor

GROUP: Theropods

WHERE IT LIVED: Argentina

WHEN IT LIVED: Late Cretaceous Period of the Mesozoic Era (90 million years ago)

LENGTH: 1.2 metres, but most of this was tail and neck. The body was the size of a chicken.

SPECIAL FEATURES: A bird-like dinosaur with feathers, long legs, wing-like limbs and a long beak-like snout. It had smaller and fewer teeth than other meat-eating dinosaurs.

FOOD: Small animals

MAIN PREDATOR: Bigger meat-eaters

DID YOU KNOW?: The long, narrow jaws and small widely-spaced teeth may mean that *Buitreraptor* probed down burrows for snakes. Scientists found fossils of snakes at the *Buitreraptor* site.

Deinonychus

Is it a bird? Is it a dinosaur? In the Cretaceous Period, some of the more active meat-eating dinosaurs were so bird-like that it is difficult to decide if they were birds or dinosaurs. *Deinonychus* was one of the most bird-like.

Deinonychus did not fly – its arms were too small to support wings. It had a heavy head, toothy jaws and a long, stiff tail to balance it as it ran. These are dinosaur features, rather than bird features.

The bones of *Deinonychus* were lightweight and hollow, just like a bird's. It had strong muscles for running or jumping. It was obviously a very active animal, and so it was probably warm-blooded. It is likely that *Deinonychus* had a feathery coat to keep it warm.

ANIMAL FACTFILE

NAME: *Deinonychus* (terrible claw)

PRONOUNCED: dye-non-ik-us

GROUP: Theropods

WHERE IT LIVED: Western USA

WHEN IT LIVED: Middle Cretaceous Period (110 to 100 million years ago)

LENGTH: 3 metres, including the long tail

SPECIAL FEATURES: Big killing claw, 12 cm long, on the hind foot, for slashing its prey

FOOD: Other dinosaurs

MAIN PREDATOR: None

DID YOU KNOW?: The fossils of several *Deinonychus* have been found surrounding those of a big plant-eater. They must have hunted this animal in packs.

73

TYRANNOSAURUS

Since its discovery about a hundred years ago, *Tyrannosaurus* has been regarded as one of the fiercest dinosaurs that ever lived. Weighing over six tonnes, *Tyrannosaurus* would have been an unstoppable force once it began to attack.

Tyrannosaurus was a fearsome hunter. The remains of duck-billed dinosaurs have been found with chunks torn out of them – in the exact shape of *Tyrannosaurus'* mouth. Fossilised *Tyrannosaurus* dung has been found, full of crunched-up bone fragments from the biggest plant-eaters of the time.

Tyrannosaurus walked on two legs with its back horizontal. Its massive jaws and killing teeth were thrust forwards, and its body was balanced by a heavy tail. This is how *Tyrannosaurus* moved about and became the terror of the last dinosaurs that ever existed.

ANIMAL FACTFILE

NAME: *Tyrannosaurus* (tyrant lizard)

PRONOUNCED: tie-ran-oh-sawr-us

GROUP: Theropods

WHERE IT LIVED: Canada and western USA

WHEN IT LIVED: Late Cretaceous Period (85 to 65 million years ago)

LENGTH: 12 metres

SPECIAL FEATURES: Huge head with forward pointing eyes to help in hunting, and tiny arms

FOOD: Other dinosaurs — especially duck-bills

MAIN PREDATOR: None

DID YOU KNOW?: It's possible that *Tyrannosaurus* was a scavenger, as well as a hunter.

MEGISTOTHERIUM

Before the evolution of modern carnivores, such as lions and bears, there was a group of predators called the creodonts. *Megistotherium* was the biggest of these, with a skull twice as long as a tiger's. It was probably the largest hunting land mammal that has ever lived.

This is the skull of a creodont. Not all creodonts were as big as *Megistotherium* – some were only the size of a weasel. But all creodonts were fierce hunters, with powerful jaws and great bone-crushing, meat-ripping teeth.

ANIMAL
FACTFILE

NAME: *Megistotherium* (the biggest beast)

PRONOUNCED: meh-jiss-toe-theer-ee-um

GROUP: Creodont mammals

WHERE IT LIVED: North Africa

WHEN IT LIVED: Mid Tertiary Period (50 to 20 million years ago)

LENGTH: 4.8 metres

SPECIAL FEATURES: The biggest meat-eating land mammal known

FOOD: Big animals like elephants

MAIN PREDATOR: None

DID YOU KNOW?: Only a single complete skull of *Megistotherium* has been found, although small pieces of other skulls have been discovered.

With a head that measured about 1.2 metres long, and a body that must have been the size of a bison, *Megistotherium* was big enough, powerful enough and fierce enough to hunt and eat elephants!

PYROTHERIUM

For most of the Tertiary Period, South America
was separated from North America by sea.
Different mammals evolved in South America,
because it was an island. Some animals looked like
those that lived on other continents, but they were
not related. *Pyrotherium* looked like an elephant.

Male *Pyrotherium* may have used
their tusks and trunks to fight with
one another to decide who was going
to mate with the females.

With its tusks and trunk, *Pyrotherium* must have looked like an elephant. It may have lived like one too, digging in the ground with its tusks, and picking up food with its short trunk.

ANIMAL FACTFILE

NAME: *Pyrotherium* (fire mammal, because its fossils were found near a volcano)

PRONOUNCED: pi-ro-theer-ee-um

GROUP: Pyrothere group of the xenungulates — the 'foreign hoofed mammals'

WHERE IT LIVED: Bolivia and Argentina

WHEN IT LIVED: Mid Tertiary Period (29 to 23 million years ago)

LENGTH: 2.7 metres

SPECIAL FEATURES: Heavy animal with a trunk and tusks

FOOD: Plants

MAIN PREDATOR: Big meat-eating marsupials

DID YOU KNOW?: *Pyrotherium* was such a mixture of different kinds of animal that it is difficult to tell what it is related to. It had the tusks and trunk of an elephant, teeth like a hippopotamus and the ear bones of a hoofed mammal.

79

UINTATHERIUM

The *Uintatherium* may have looked like a rhinoceros, with its big heavy body and horns, but they are not related. Many rhinoceros-like mammals lived in early Tertiary times. They probably evolved to take the place of horned dinosaurs like *Triceratops*, that had only just become extinct.

Uintatherium weighed something like two tonnes, and carried itself on massive elephant-like legs. It was probably only the males that had the metre-long tusks. They may have used them to scare other animals.

Uintatherium must have looked very frightening. It had six horns on its head and a pair of sharp tusks in its upper jaw. However, it was a gentle plant-eater.

ANIMAL
FACTFILE

NAME: *Uintatherium* (mammal from the Uinta Mountains in the USA)

PRONOUNCED: you-in-ta-theer-ee-um

GROUP: Uintatheres

WHERE IT LIVED: Utah, USA

WHEN IT LIVED: Early Tertiary Period (40 to 35 million years ago)

LENGTH: 4 metres

SPECIAL FEATURES: Three pairs of horns and a pair of sharp tusks

FOOD: Plants

MAIN PREDATOR: None

DID YOU KNOW?: In the 1870s two American palaeontologists, Othniel Marsh and Edward Cope, argued bitterly over who should name this animal. It was finally named *Uintatherium* by another palaeontologist, Joseph Leidy, in 1872.

INDRICOTHERIUM

This massive beast is an ancient relative of the rhinoceros. Unlike modern rhinoceroses, it did not have a horn on its nose. An animal this size would not need a weapon to defend itself. It is the biggest land mammal ever to have lived.

As can be seen from this fossil, *Indricotherium* had two pairs of teeth at the front of the mouth. It also had two tusk-like teeth on the upper jaw that pointed downwards and two on the lower jaw that pointed forwards. Together, they were used for scraping leaves and twigs from high branches to eat.

ANIMAL
FACTFILE

NAME: *Indricotherium* (mammal of Indrik – a monster of local legends)

PRONOUNCED: in-drik-oh-theer-ee-um

GROUP: Perissodactyls (odd-toed hoofed mammals)

WHERE IT LIVED: Pakistan

WHEN IT LIVED: Mid Tertiary Period (20 to 30 million years ago)

LENGTH: 8 metres long, and 4.5 metres tall at the shoulder. An elephant is about 7 metres long and 3 metres tall at the shoulder.

SPECIAL FEATURES: The biggest land mammal that we know of

FOOD: Leaves and twigs

MAIN PREDATOR: None

DID YOU KNOW?: *Indricotherium* must have weighed about 10 tonnes.

Although *Indricotherium* was like a rhinoceros, it lived more like a giraffe. Its long legs, on three-toed feet, held its body high above the ground. The tall neck and the head (which was over a metre long) reached to the tops of the highest trees.

83

BASILOSAURUS

One of the earliest whales was *Basilosaurus*. Like all whales, it was a mammal. Although mammals evolved on land, many of them returned to the sea at the beginning of the Tertiary Period. The giant sea reptiles had become extinct, and sea-living mammals evolved to take their place.

Like the whales of today, *Basilosaurus* would have needed to come to the surface to breathe. It had nostrils at the tip of its nose, rather than a blowhole on top of its head as modern whales do.

ANIMAL
FACTFILE

NAME: *Basilosaurus* (emperor lizard)

PRONOUNCED: bass-il-oh-sawr-us

GROUP: Archaeocete whales

WHERE IT LIVED: All the oceans

WHEN IT LIVED: Early Tertiary Period (45 to 35 million years ago)

LENGTH: 18 metres

SPECIAL FEATURES: A long, thin and flexible body, ideal for catching fish

FOOD: Fish and cephalopods

MAIN PREDATOR: Maybe sharks

DID YOU KNOW?: Although it is a mammal, *Basilosaurus* has a name like a dinosaur. This is because the first scientist to find its fossils thought that they came from a giant reptile.

This fossil shows the long, snake-like backbone of *Basilosaurus*. Over a hundred years ago, someone stuck several bones together from different skeletons and tried to pass it off as a sea serpent.

DESMOSTYLUS

This hippopotamus-like animal with strange crooked legs lived around the edge of the Pacific Ocean in mid-Tertiary times. It probably used its tusks and heavy teeth to root about on the shallow sea floor for shellfish, or perhaps it grazed on seaweeds. It was such an odd animal that scientists are not sure what it ate!

This is a fossil of a *Desmostylus* tooth. From the chemicals in its bones, scientists have worked out that it spent most of its time in water – by the shore or in river mouths.

ANIMAL FACTFILE

NAME: *Desmostylus* (chain-tooth, after the way the back teeth are linked together)

PRONOUNCED: des-mo-sty-lus

GROUP: Desmostylid mammals

WHERE IT LIVED: Coasts of Japan and California, USA

WHEN IT LIVED: Mid to Late Tertiary Period (14 to 19 million years ago)

LENGTH: 1.8 metres

SPECIAL FEATURES: A lumbering semi-aquatic mammal with powerful teeth

FOOD: Shellfish or seaweed

MAIN PREDATOR: Sharks

DID YOU KNOW?: The nearest living relative of *Desmostylus* is the elephant.

The inwardly-turned feet of *Desmostylus* made it very clumsy while walking on land. Underwater, though, it would have been very graceful. It could walk across the sea bed as a hippopotamus does in African rivers today.

GOMPHOTHERIUM

Elephants existed for most of the Tertiary Period. They started as small pig-like animals, but soon developed into big beasts with tusks and trunks. Many types of elephants evolved with different arrangements of tusks. *Gomphotherium* was an elephant with four tusks.

The tusks on the lower jaw of *Gomphotherium* made the jaw very long and spade-like. The tusks were used for rooting in the forest floor, or in the beds of streams and lakes looking for food.

We do not know for sure if *Gomphotherium* had a trunk because trunks are made of flesh that does not fossilise. However, the short neck shows that the head could not reach the ground. The skull shows features similar to the trunk area of modern elephants. As a result, scientists think the *Gomphotherium* probably had a trunk.

ANIMAL
FACTFILE

NAME: *Gomphotherium* (bolted mammal)

PRONOUNCED: gomp-foe-theer-ee-um

GROUP: Elephants

WHERE IT LIVED: Europe, Kenya, Pakistan, Japan and North America

WHEN IT LIVED: Late Tertiary Period (23 to 3 million years ago)

LENGTH: 4 metres

SPECIAL FEATURES: Elephant with a pair of tusks on the upper jaw and another on the lower

FOOD: Plants

MAIN PREDATOR: None

DID YOU KNOW?: *Gomphotherium* probably evolved in Africa and then spread to the rest of the world.

DEINOTHERIUM

Modern elephants have their tusks on the upper jaw. *Deinotherium* had its tusks on the lower jaw and they turned downwards. These tusks would have been used as picks for digging up roots and other ground vegetation.

Deinotherium is the second biggest land animal known, after *Indricotherium*. It existed for almost 20 million years – a very long time.

The early discovery of *Deinotherium* skulls on the Greek Islands may have led to the legend of the Cyclops – the one-eyed giant. The nostrils in the skull are fused into a single hole, which looks like an enormous eye socket.

ANIMAL FACTFILE

NAME: *Deinotherium* (terrible mammal)

PRONOUNCED: dy-no-theer-ee-um

GROUP: Elephants

WHERE IT LIVED: Africa and Southern Europe

WHEN IT LIVED: Late Tertiary Period (20 to 2 million years ago)

HEIGHT: 4 metres at the shoulders

SPECIAL FEATURES: Down-curved tusks on the lower jaw

FOOD: Plants

MAIN PREDATOR: None

DID YOU KNOW?: *Deinotherium* was around at the same time as our earliest human ancestors.

AMPHICYON

Amphicyon was as big as a grizzly bear. It was one of the largest hunting animals in Middle Tertiary times. With its massive body and powerful legs it could hunt down most of the animals that were around, and kill them with its sharp dog-like teeth.

The legs of *Amphicyon* were short, and it walked on flat feet, like a bear. It could not have run fast. It probably hunted its prey by ambushing it, rather than running it down.

The *Amphicyon* is neither a bear nor a dog, but something in between. The amphicyonids were the main hunters of the Middle Tertiary, and ranged from the size of badgers to the size of the biggest bears.

ANIMAL
FACTFILE

NAME: *Amphicyon* (nearly a dog)

PRONOUNCED: am-fee-sy-on

GROUP: Amphicyonids – the bear dogs

WHERE IT LIVED: Europe and North America

WHEN IT LIVED: Mid Tertiary Period (30 to 14 million years ago)

HEIGHT: 1 metre

SPECIAL FEATURES: Skeleton like that of a bear, but teeth like that of a dog

FOOD: Other animals, particularly the small horses of the time

MAIN PREDATOR: None

DID YOU KNOW?: The bear-dogs took over from the creodonts in the early part of the Tertiary Period, and were then replaced by the canids (wolves, foxes and dogs) in the later part.

93

MEGALANIA

When the first people arrived in Australia 40,000 years ago, they must have been terrified by *Megalania*. This gigantic lizard was the size of a lion. It was a fierce predator, with sharp teeth and big claws. It would have hunted by ambush, lying in wait until its prey came close, then leaping out to attack.

Megalania may have hunted in short bursts of speed. Like other reptiles, *Megalania* could not control its body temperature, and so it would have over-heated if it tried to run too fast for too long.

Scientists have not yet found a full skeleton of *Megalania*. The individual bones that have been found suggest that it had quite a short tail, and a massive body.

ANIMAL
FACTFILE

NAME: *Megalania* (great ripper)

PRONOUNCED: meg-al-ai-nee-ah

GROUP: Varanid lizards

WHERE IT LIVED: Australia

WHEN IT LIVED: Early Quaternary Period (1.6 million to 40,000 years ago)

LENGTH: 5.5 metres

SPECIAL FEATURES: The biggest lizard that has ever existed

FOOD: Meat, either from animals it caught itself, or scavenged from the bodies of those that were already dead

MAIN PREDATOR: Carnivorous marsupials, such as *Thylacoleo*

DID YOU KNOW?: *Megalania* would have tackled prey up to ten times its own weight. That means that it could have hunted the biggest animals in Australia at that time.

DINORNIS

Before early people reached New Zealand, about 1,000 years ago, bats were the only mammals living there. However, there was a vast range of ground-dwelling birds known as the moas. The biggest of these was *Dinornis*. It was the heaviest bird to have ever lived.

When you see a moa skeleton in a museum, it often has its head held high. In life it would usually have held its head close to the ground, where the food was. It would have looked up to scan for danger.

During the Quaternary Period, New Zealand was covered in forest. *Dinornis* had a short, broad beak. It was ideal for rooting about in thick forest undergrowth to find the tastiest food.

ANIMAL FACTFILE

NAME: *Dinornis* (terrible bird)

PRONOUNCED: die-nor-nis

GROUP: Ratites – flightless birds

WHERE IT LIVED: New Zealand

WHEN IT LIVED: Throughout the Quaternary Period (1.6 million to 200 years ago)

HEIGHT: 2 metres at the mid-point of the back

SPECIAL FEATURES: Giant flightless bird with a tiny head and enormous legs

FOOD: Twigs, berries and leaves. It also swallowed stones to help to grind up the food.

MAIN PREDATOR: People, and a kind of giant eagle that lived in New Zealand

DID YOU KNOW?: There were 11 different species of moa, some only the size of a turkey. Humans hunted moas to extinction a few hundred years ago.

MEGALOCEROS

Modern moose and elk have spectacular antlers. However, these are tiny compared with the antlers of the big Ice Age deer *Megaloceros*. Each antler would have been about 1.5 metres – longer than you are! Only male deer had antlers. They used them to attract a mate and fight off rivals.

Megaloceros lived in many European countries, but it was particularly common in Ireland, where there were no predators and plenty of food. The antlers of *Megaloceros* are often found in Irish peat bogs. For this reason, it is also known as the Great Irish Elk.

The leader of the *Megaloceros* herd must have been a magnificent sight, watching over his herd and protecting it against other males. However, it could not guard against the hunting skills of early humans. By the end of the Ice Age, *Megaloceros* was hunted to extinction.

ANIMAL FACTFILE

NAME: *Megaloceros* (giant horn)

PRONOUNCED: meg-ah-loss-er-oss

GROUP: Artiodactyls

WHERE IT LIVED: Europe and Western Asia

WHEN IT LIVED: Mid Quaternary Period (1.5 million to 11,000 years ago)

HEIGHT: 3 metres

SPAN OF ANTLERS: 3.3 metres. Today, the largest moose antlers have a span of about 2 metres.

SPECIAL FEATURES: Enormous antlers that were shed and regrown every year

FOOD: Grass and low-growing vegetation

MAIN PREDATOR: Early humans

DID YOU KNOW?: *Megaloceros* needed large amounts of minerals to grow its antlers every year. About 11,000 years ago the climate became colder and the vegetation that provided these minerals became less common. Climate change, together with hunting by early humans, led to *Megaloceros'* extinction.

MAMMUTHUS

Probably the most familiar of the Ice Age
mammals is the woolly mammoth, with
its long shaggy hair and massive curved
tusks. Unlike today's elephants that
live in hot countries, the mammoth
was adapted to the cold.

Sometimes mammoths became buried in mud when they sank into a peat bog, or when a riverbank collapsed on them. This mud later froze. As a result, we sometimes find complete frozen bodies of mammoths, thousands of years old.

ANIMAL FACTFILE

NAME: *Mammuthus* (burrowing one)

PRONOUNCED: mam-uth-us

GROUP: Elephants

WHERE IT LIVED: Canada, Alaska, Siberia and Northern Europe

WHEN IT LIVED: Late Tertiary Period to Late Quaternary Period (4.8 million years ago to 2,500 years ago)

HEIGHT: 2.7 metres at the shoulders

SPECIAL FEATURES: Adaptations to living in a cold climate

FOOD: Grasses, lichens and mosses

MAIN PREDATOR: Humans

DID YOU KNOW?: Mammoths were named 'burrowing one' because when their bones were first found in Siberia, the local people thought that they were the remains of animals that lived underground.

The thick hair of the mammoth protected it from the cold. The hump on its shoulders contained a food supply of fat that would see it through the harsh winters. The huge curving tusks were used as snowploughs, for scraping snow away from the mosses, lichens and grasses on which it fed.

COELODONTA

The woolly rhinoceros, *Coelodonta*, is one of the most familiar Ice Age mammals. It roamed the freezing northern plains, either on its own or in small family groups. Like the mammoth, it was well-adapted to cold conditions, even though its modern relatives live in tropical areas.

Coelodonta had many adaptations that helped keep it warm. It was covered in shaggy hair. It also had short legs and small ears, so these parts of its body did not get so cold.

The nose of *Coelodonta* had a bony structure to support the weight of its horn, which was made of compacted hair. Both males and females had horns. They used them to push away snow, to reach the grass underneath.

ANIMAL
FACTFILE

NAME: *Coelodonta* (hollow tooth)

PRONOUNCED: see-low-dont-ah

GROUP: Perissodactyls

WHERE IT LIVED: Northern Europe and Asia

WHEN IT LIVED: Early to Mid Quaternary Period (1.8 million to 20,000 years ago)

LENGTH: 3.3 metres

SPECIAL FEATURES: Two horns, one of which was 1 metre long

FOOD: Grass

MAIN PREDATOR: Humans

DID YOU KNOW?: Early people hunted the woolly rhinoceros and drew pictures of it on cave walls in central Europe.

SMILODON

The sabre-tooth cats were the main hunters of big animals during Quaternary times. A sabre is a curved sword, and that is exactly what *Smilodon*'s long front teeth were like. They could easily slash through thick skin and muscle. There were many types of sabre-tooth, and *Smilodon* was the biggest.

Smilodon's powerful jaw is obvious in this skull. The canine teeth were very long and used as killing weapons. They killed by slashing their prey, not biting it as modern cats do.

ANIMAL FACTFILE

NAME: *Smilodon* (sabre toothed)

PRONOUNCED: smy-lo-don

GROUP: Machairodont group of the cats

WHERE IT LIVED: North America

WHEN IT LIVED: Early to Mid Quaternary Period (1.6 million to 11,000 years ago)

LENGTH: 1.5 metres

SPECIAL FEATURES: 15 cm canine teeth and strong neck muscles to drive them downwards with force

FOOD: Big mammals like elephants, horses and bison

MAIN PREDATOR: None

DID YOU KNOW?: Many complete skeletons of *Smilodon* have been found in Los Angeles, USA. The animals became stuck in the tar pits there.

Smilodon was not a fast runner. Instead, it ambushed its prey and wounded it fatally. It would have then waited for the injured animal to bleed to death before eating it.

GIGANTOPITHECUS

The fierce *Gigantopithecus* could rear up to a great height, and bellow loudly. It was the biggest ape that ever lived. *Gigantopithecus* made its home in the forested foothills of the mountains of China.

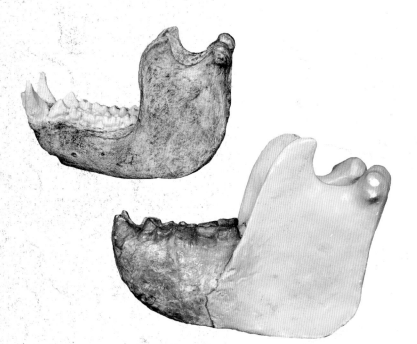

This picture shows a model of the jaw bone of *Gigantopithecus* (bottom) compared to the jaw bone of a gorilla (top). *Gigantopithecus* is very much bigger. All that scientists really know about *Gigantopithecus* is the size of its teeth. From the teeth, scientists can put together the appearance of the whole animal.

ANIMAL
FACTFILE

NAME: *Gigantopithecus* (giant ape)

PRONOUNCED: ji-gan-toe-pith-a-kuss

GROUP: Apes

WHERE IT LIVED: China

WHEN IT LIVED: Late Tertiary Period to Early Quaternary Period (13 million to 500,000 years ago)

HEIGHT: 3 metres

SPECIAL FEATURES: Large teeth for chewing the tough mountain vegetation

FOOD: Bamboo and other plants

MAIN PREDATOR: Not known

DID YOU KNOW?: *Gigantopithecus* was first discovered in 1935, when a German paleontologist found fossil teeth for sale in a Chinese medicine shop. He realised the teeth came from a primate that had never before been identified.

There is a theory that *Gigantopithecus* is still alive. Some people believe it is the Yeti, or abominable snowman, said to live in the Himalayas.

ANIMAL FAMILIES GLOSSARY

Ammonites — a group of sea-living cephalopods common in the seas of dinosaur times. They were like squid but in coiled shells, and the shells of each species were all quite different from one another. Many can be found as fossils today.

Amphicyonids — the bear-dogs. These were meat-eating mammals from the Late Tertiary that were related both to the bears and the dogs.

Arthropods — invertebrates with an outside shell and jointed legs. They include the modern insects, crabs and spiders. The shell is made of material like your fingernails.

Cephalopods — literally the "head-footed" animals. The modern types, the octopus and squid, appear to have legs branching from their faces. In prehistoric times many of them had chambered shells.

Creodonts — a group of early meat-eating mammals from the Early Tertiary. Although they resembled modern wolves, weasels and bears, they were not related to them.

Gorgonopsians — a fierce group of mammal-like reptiles, looking like a cross between a crocodile and a sabre-toothed tiger, living mainly in late Permian times.

Graptolites — a group of tiny sea-living animals that consisted of a string of individuals attached to a stalk. They floated in the waters of the Ordovician and Silurian seas.

Ichthyosaurs — a group of sea-going reptiles. They were well-adapted to living in the sea and looked like dolphins or sharks. They had fins on the tail and back and paddles for limbs. Ichthyosaurs were common in the Triassic and the Jurassic Periods but died out in the Cretaceous.

Labyrinthodonts — one of the groups of early amphibians, from the Carboniferous and Permian Periods. They were so-called because the enamel of the teeth was contorted like a labyrinth, or maze.

Machairodonts — the group of sabre-toothed cats. The canine teeth were very long and used as killing weapons. They killed by slashing their prey, not biting it as modern cats do.

Marginocephalians — the plant-eating dinosaurs group that had ornamented heads. The ornaments were sometimes horns and neck shields, and sometimes were domes of bone used as battering rams.

Marsupials — a major group of mammals that carry their young in pouches. Nowadays they are confined to Australia, except for the opossum of the Americas. In the Tertiary Period many of the hunting animals of South America as well as Australia were marsupials.

Mosasaurs — a group of sea reptiles from the Late Cretaceous Period. They were very much like swimming lizards with paddles instead of feet. Indeed they were very closely related to the monitor lizards of today.

Nothosaurs — sea reptiles that had long jaws for catching fish, and webbed feet for swimming through water. Several kinds of nothosaur lived in the shallow waters around Europe and Asia in the Triassic Period.

Ornithopods — the plant-eating dinosaurs group that usually went about on two legs. They were present throughout the Late Triassic and Jurassic Periods but it was in the later Cretaceous that they became really important.

Pelycosaurs — the most primitive group of the mammal-like reptiles, from early Permian times. Most of them had big fins on their backs. Some were meat-eaters and others were plant-eaters.

Perissodactyls — the group of odd-toed hoofed mammals. Modern forms include the horse, the rhinoceros and the tapir. They normally have either one toe or three on the foot. The other hoofed mammal group are the artiodactyls — the even-toed hoofed mammals.

Placodonts — a group of swimming reptiles that fed on shellfish. Many had shells like turtles, although they were not related.

Plesiosaurs — the group of swimming reptiles with the paddle-shaped limbs and flat bodies. There were two types — the long-necked type and the whale-like short-necked type. They lived throughout dinosaur times.

Primates — the group of mammals that includes the lemurs, the monkeys, the apes and ourselves. Primates have hands and forward-facing eyes.

Prosauropods — an early dinosaur group that were plant-eaters and had long necks for reaching into trees. They were the biggest animals of the Triassic and early Jurassic, but not as big as their descendants — the sauropods.

Pterodactyloids — one of the two group of pterosaurs. These had short tails and long necks, unlike the other group, the rhamphorhynchoids, that had long tails and short necks.

Pterosaurs — the flying reptiles of the age of dinosaurs. They had broad leathery wings supported on a long fourth finger, and were covered in hair to keep them warm.

Pyrotheres — a group of xenungulates that resembled the modern elephant although they were not closely related to elephants. They lived in South America in the mid-Tertiary Period.

Ratites — the group of flightless birds. Modern types include the emu and cassowary of Australia, the ostrich of Africa and the rhea of South America.

Rauisuchians — a group of land-living meat-eaters of the Triassic Period, closely related to the crocodiles. They were the fiercest animals of the time.

Sauropods — the plant-eating dinosaurs group that had huge bodies, long necks and long tails. They were the biggest land-living animals that ever lived, and reached their peak in late Jurassic times.

Spinosaurids — a type of theropod dinosaur.

Therapsids — the most mammal-like group of the mammal-like reptiles. They were covered in fur and had teeth like the teeth of a mammal. Some were so mammal-like that you would think they were dogs.

Theropods — the meat-eating dinosaurs group. They all had the same shape: long jaws with sharp teeth, strong hind legs, smaller front legs with clawed hands, and a small body balanced by a long tail.

Thyreophorans — the armoured dinosaurs group. There were two main lines. The first to develop were the plated stegosaurs, and later came the armour-covered ankylosaurs.

Trilobites — a group of common sea-living arthropods, common from Cambrian to Devonian times, that had head shields, tail shields, and the body divided into segments in between.

Tyrannosaurs— one of the theropod dinosaur groups. At the end of the Cretaceous Period they were amongst the biggest meat-eaters of all time, but the early forms, in the late Jurassic, were quite small animals.

Uintatheres — a group of heavy, rhinoceros-like mammals from the Early Tertiary Period. They had several pairs of horn-like structures on the head and a pair of long tusks.

Varanids — the group of lizards that include the modern monitor lizards, such as the Komodo dragon. Prehistoric forms include the swimming mosasaurs from the Cretaceous Period and the lion-sized lizards that lived in Australia during the Quaternary Period.

Xenungulates — a group of hoofed mammals that lived in South America during the Tertiary Period. They were not related to the hoofed mammals of the rest of the world but evolved independently.

GLOSSARY

Abominable Snowman — an imaginary hairy ape, said to live in the Himalayan Mountains.

Adapted — changing to survive in a particular habitat or weather conditions.

Ambushing — lying in wait out of sight, and then making a surprise attack.

Amphibian — an animal that is able to live on both land and water.

Ancestor — an early form of the animal group that lived in the past.

Blowhole — a hole at the top of a whale's head that is its nostril. To breathe, a whale comes to the surface of the water and blows air out of the hole and breathes air in. When the whale is underwater, a flap of skin covers the hole.

Canines — strong, pointed teeth.

Carnivore — a meat-eating animal.

Carrion — the meat left over from a dead animal.

Cephalopod — an animal that lives in the sea and which has a big head and tentacles, such as an octopus.

Ceratopsian dinosaur — a type of dinosaur that had frills, spikes and horns as protection.

Cold-blooded — animals, such as reptiles or amphibians, which rely on their environment to control their body temperature.

Colony — a group of animals of the same kind living closely together.

Compacted hair — a batch of hair that is squashed together so tightly it becomes hard.

Continent — one of the world's main land masses, such as Africa and Europe.

Cunning — clever at getting what they want.

Dinosaur — large group of meat-eating or plant-eating

reptiles that no longer exist.

Duck-bill — a type of dinosaur that had a beak which looked like a duck's beak or bill.

Evolution — changes or developments that happen to all forms of life over millions of years, as a result of changes in the environment.

Evolutionary line — the different stages in the development of a certain type of animal.

Evolve — to change or develop through time.

Extinct — an animal group which no longer exists.

Flexible — can move in all directions easily.

Fossil — the remains of a prehistoric plant or animal that has been buried for a long time and become hardened in rock.

Fossilised — turned into a fossil.

Grinding teeth — these are teeth used to chew food.

Ice age — a period of time when the Earth was covered in ice.

Incisor — sharp-edged front tooth in the upper and lower jaws.

Hollow bones — bones that have a space inside them so that they are not solid. Hollow bones are much lighter than solid bones.

Lagoon — a shallow pond joined to seas or lakes.

Lichen — a type of plant like moss.

Mammal — a warm-blooded animal which is covered in hair. The female gives birth to live young and produces milk from her own body to feed them.

Marsupial — an animal such as a kangaroo, which has a pouch on the front of its body in which it carries its young.

Meat-shearing teeth — special teeth that are used to cut or slice the flesh from bones.

Minerals — found in food and help to keep the body working well.

Molars — special teeth used for grinding food.

Moose — a type of deer from North America.

Nipping teeth — these are teeth used to bite leaves off the trees.

Oases — green areas in a desert, where there is water and where plants grow.

Open plain — a wide space without trees.

Organic matter — really tiny animal or plant life.

Ornithopod — a type of plant-eating dinosaur.

Paleontologist — a scientist who studies fossils.

Palaeozoic Era — the period when life first appeared on Earth.

Peat bog — a type of ground that is damp and covered in moss.

Plesiosaur — a reptile which lived in the sea.

Pouch — a pocket-shaped part of the body.

Predator — an animal that hunts and kills other animals for food.

Prehistory — a time before humans evolved.

Prey — animals that are hunted by other animals as food.

Primitive — a very early stage in the development of a species.

Prosauropod — late Triassic Period ancestors of long-necked, plant-eating dinosaurs.

Quarry — a place where stones are dug up for building.

Reef — a ridge of rock, sand or coral near the surface of the sea.

Reptile — a cold-blooded, crawling or creeping animal with a backbone.

Reptilian — animals that look like a reptile.

River mouth — the place where a river flows into the sea.

Rock painting — a drawing made by our early ancestors millions of years ago.

Sauropod — a large plant-eating dinosaur.

Scavenger — an animal that feeds off food other animals have hunted.

Segmented — divided into separate parts.

Semi-aquatic — animals which spend a lot of time in water but which need air to breathe, for example, turtles, otters and frogs.

Serrated — having a jagged edge like a saw.

Snout — an animal's nose.

Soared — flew high in the sky.

Species — a group of animals which all look like each other.

Spine — the backbone of an animal.

Streamlined — a smooth, bullet-shaped body that makes it easy for the animal to move through the air or water.

Tar pit — an area where thick, black, sticky liquid just under the ground bubbles up to the top.

Trilobite — an early type of sea animal that no longer exists.

Tropic(al) — a place that is close to the Equator and which has a hot, wet climate.

Tusk — a long pointed tooth which grows outside of an animal's mouth.

Tyrannosaur — a type of large meat-eating dinosaur.

Vertebrae — small bones which form the spine.

Warm-blooded — animals, such as small mammals, which always have the same body temperature.

Well-preserved — a fossil which is in good condition.

Wing membrane — a thin sheet of skin attached to bone which forms a wing.

Wingspan — the length of a bird's wings, from the tip of one to the tip of the other.

INDEX